Copyright © 2010 by Diane Rollman. 86903-ROLL

ISBN: Softcover 978-1-4535-7791-2
Hardcover 978-1-4535-7792-9

All rights reserved. No part of this book may be reproduced or transmitted in any form or by any means, electronic or mechanical, including photocopying, recording, or by any information storage and retrieval system, without permission
in writing from the copyright owner.

This is a work of fiction. Names, characters, places and incidents either are the product of the author's imagination or are used fictitiously, and any resemblance to any actual persons, living or dead, events, or locales is entirely coincidental.

This book was printed in the United States of America.

To order additional copies of this book, contact:
Xlibris Corporation
1-888-795-4274
www.Xlibris.com
Orders@Xlibris.com

Hello, my name is Keaton. This is my family. I do everything with them.

Here I am hanging out with the girls and their friends.

I love when we have company.
Sometimes the parties get
really crowded.

Then one day, everything seemed to change. Mom was telling Dad and the girls that Aunt Diane was coming for a visit next week. All at once they started asking questions "What about Keaton?" "Where are we going to put Keaton?"

"What about Keaton?" I asked myself. "Who is Aunt Diane? What did I ever do to her?"

For the next few days everyone cleaned and fussed in preparation of Aunt Diane's arrival. "She must be very important." I thought. "Maybe a queen or a moviestar!"

On the day she was to arrive, Mom announced that Keaton would be kept in the laundry room. The girls gathered my bowls, toy mouse, favorite rug, and litter box . Then, they brought it all , including me, into the laundry room and closed the door.

"Aunt Diane must be a mean old witch that only likes black cats. Or maybe she's a monster that chases cats."

When the doorbell rang, everyone rushed to the door to greet Aunt Diane. I could hear their voices. They sounded happy and excited. "How could they be so eager to see a mean old witch?"

Then, I heard "her" voice. It sounded sweet and loving. "How could a monster have such a kind voice?"

All afternoon I could hear
them telling stories and
laughing. I was very confused.
"Why couldn't I be there?"

After dinner everyone seemed to settle down. I heard footsteps coming. It didn't sound like Mom or Dad. It wasn't the girls. "Oh no, it's her!" Aunt Diane was walking toward the laundry room.

" Hello Keaton." I heard in the sweet, loving voice. " I am Aunt Diane. I am sorry you must stay in the laundry room during my visit. You see, I have serious allergies especially to cat dander. If you were to be out and about I would sneeze constantly. My eyes would get red and watery. I would be a terrible mess, unable to stay for more than an hour. I have heard such wonderful stories about you from the family. I appreciate what you are doing for me and just had to come and thank you myself."

The next morning after breakfast, I could hear everyone rushing around. When Mom announced that the taxi had arrived, they all gathered at the door to say goodbye. It sounded like a mix of laughing and crying at the same time; and then I heard the sweet, loving voice call out "Goodbye Keaton, and thank you again."

The minute the taxi drove away the girls came running to the laundry room. They were as happy to see me as I was to see them. They told me how much they missed me and thanked me for helping the family. Even Mom and Dad bought me a special treat.

Everything is back to normal again. I love being a part of a family.

Edwards Brothers,Inc!
Thorofare, NJ 08086
28 March, 2011
BA2011087